100 NO-COOK RECIPES

LENA ALEX

To order additional copies of this book, contact:
Xlibris
844-714-8691
www.Xlibris.com
Orders@Xlibris.com

ISBN: 978-1-6641-8010-9 (sc)
ISBN: 978-1-6641-8009-3 (e)

Print information available on the last page

Rev. date: 06/18/2021

No-cook recipes, 3 min. make from ready to eat ingredients
Time savers, super simple.
Food is fun. Food is life.

ENJOY!

Directions for all recipes:

chop and mix

Makes 4 servings

Contents

Crab Meat Recipes

1. Crab meat (imitation) 1 pack 8oz
   Artichoke Hearts marinated 6oz
   Cucumber pickled medium size
   White onion small size
   Celery ½ of stem
   Mayonnaise 2 tablespoons

2. Crab meat (imitation) 1 pack 8oz
   Olives black ½ of can 6oz
   Tangerines 2
   Celery ½ of stem

3. Crab meat (imitation) 1 pack 8oz
   Beats canned 7 slices
   Red caviar 2 tablespoons
   Corn sweet ½ of can 15.25oz

4. Crab meat (imitation) 1 pack 8oz
   Apples 2
   Cucumber fresh medium size
   Sweet red pepper 1

5. Crab meat (imitation) 1 pack 8oz
   King's Hawaiian bread 4 bans
   Honey 2 tablespoons
   Grapes 1 LB

6. Crab meat (imitation) 1 pack 8oz
   Pineapple ½
   Corn sweet ½ of can 15.25oz
   Cheese Queso Oaxaca 3oz

7. Crab meat (imitation) 1 pack 8oz
   Banana 1
   Crackers 10 pieces
   Oranges

8. Crab meat (imitation) 1 pack 8oz
   Salmon smocked 1 pack 3oz
   Cucumber fresh medium size
   Salad spring mix 2 cups

9. Crab meat canned 5oz
   Apples 2
   Artichoke Hearts marinated 6oz
   Cucumber fresh medium size
   Crackers 10 pieces

Pink Salmon Recipes

10. Pink salmon can 14.75oz
    Apples 2
    Cucumber fresh medium size
    Salad Iceberg Garden 2 cups
    Crackers 15 pieces

11. Pink salmon can 14.75oz
    Olives black ½ of can 6oz
    Celery ½ of stem
    White onion small size
    Crackers 15 pieces

12. Pink salmon can 14.75oz
    Mushrooms marinated 5oz
    Tomatoes fresh 2
    Corn sweet ½ of can 15.25oz
    Salad Italian Crunchy Blends 2 cups

Smoked Salmon Recipes

13. Smoked salmon 1 pack 3oz
    Avocados 2
    Cheese Queso Oaxaca 3oz
    Crackers 15 pieces

14. Smoked salmon 1 pack 3oz
    Cucumber fresh medium size
    Olives black ½ of can 6oz
    Onion white small size

15. Smoked salmon 1 pack 3oz
    Apples 2
    Red pepper sweet 1
    Corn sweet ½ of can 15.25oz

Red Caviar Recipes

16. Red caviar (canned) 3 tablespoons
Artichoke Hearts marinated 6oz
King's Hawaiian bread 4 bans
Radish 1 bunch

17. Red caviar (canned) 3 tablespoons
Beats marinated 7 slices
Beans 1 can 15.5oz
Cucumber fresh medium size

18. Red caviar (canned) 3 tablespoons
Hummus 1 jar 10oz
Cucumber fresh medium size
Red pepper sweet 1

19. Red caviar (canned) 3 tablespoons
Cheese Gouda 2oz
Beans 1 can 15.5oz
Pears 2

Black Caviar Recipes

20. Black caviar (canned) 4 tablespoons
King's Hawaiian bread 4 bans
Black olives 1 can 6oz
Tomato juice 3 cups

21. Black caviar (canned) 4 tablespoons
Sausage 6oz
Celery ½ of stem
Crackers 10 pieces

22. Black caviar (canned) 4 tablespoons
Mangos 3
Hummus 1 jar 10oz
Cilantro 4 stems

Shrimp Recipes

23. Shrimp cooked 3 cups
Tomatoes 3
Mango 3
Celery ½ of stem
Salad Iceberg Garden 2 cups

24. Shrimp cooked 3 cups
Banana 1
Apples 2
Raspberry 1 pack 6oz
Corn sweet ½ of can 15.25oz

25. Shrimp cooked 3 cups
Artichoke Hearts marinated 6oz
Cheese Queso Oaxaca 2oz
Onion white small size
Salad Spring mix 2 cups

26. Shrimp cooked 4 cups
Cranberry sauce 2 tablespoons
Celery ½ of stem
Crackers 10 pieces

Tuna Recipes

27. Tuna 1 can 12.5oz
    Green peas ½ of can 15oz
    Tangerines 3
    Crackers 10 pieces
    Olive oil 1 tablespoon

28. Tuna 1 can 12.5oz
    Beats marinated 7 slices
    King's Hawaiian bread 4 bans
    Cucumber fresh medium size

29. Tuna 1 can 12.5oz
    Apples 3
    Corn sweet ½ of can 15.25oz
    Crackers 12 pieces

30. Tuna 1 can 12.5oz
    Beats marinated 7 slices
    Olives black ½ of can 6oz
    Celery ½ of stem

Mushroom Recipes

31. Mushrooms marinated 4.5oz
    Cucumber fresh medium size
    Olives black ½ of can 6oz
    Onion white small size
    Olive oil 1 tablespoon

32. Mushrooms marinated 4.5oz
    Beans 1 can 15.5oz
    Corn sweet ½ of can 15.25oz
    Olives black ½ of can 6oz
    Onion sweet small size
    Olive oil 1 tablespoon

33. Mushrooms marinated 4.5oz
Artichoke Hearts marinated 6oz
Cucumber medium size
Salad Italian Crunchy Blends 2 cups

34. Mushrooms marinated 4.5oz
Tangerines 3
Red pepper sweet 1
Cucumber fresh 1 medium size
Green peas ½ of can 15oz

35. Mushrooms marinated 4.5oz
Salami 2oz
Avocados 2
Artichoke Hearts marinated 6oz

Salami Recipes

36. Salami 2oz
King's Hawaiian bread 4 bans
Cheese Queso Oaxaca 3oz
Celery ½ of stem
Onion white small size

37. Salami 2oz
Beans 1 can 15.5oz
Red pepper sweet 1
Cucumber fresh medium size

38. Salami 2oz
Mushrooms marinated 4.5oz
Artichoke Hearts marinated 6oz
Lettuce 2 cups
Green peas ½ of can 15oz

39. Salami 2oz
Strawberry 10oz
Olives black ½ of can 6oz
Lettuce 2 cups

Sausage Recipes

40. Sausage 6oz
    Avocados 2
    Olives black ½ of can 6oz

41. Sausage 6oz
    Cucumber fresh medium size
    Olives black ½ of can 6oz
    Crackers 10
    Tomato souse 1 cup

42. Sausage 6oz
    Artichoke Hearts marinated 6oz
    Cucumber fresh medium size
    Salad Iceberg Garden 12oz

43. Sausage 6oz
    King's Hawaiian bread 4 bans
    Beats marinated 5 slices
    Cucumber pickled medium size

44. Sausage 6oz
    Red pepper sweet 1
    Radish 1 bunch
    Salad Spring mix 2 cups

45. Sausage 6oz
    Cheese Queso Oaxaca 2oz
    Cucumber fresh medium size
    Cranberry souse 2 tablespoons

46. Sausage 6oz
    Orange 1
    Romaine Hearts 4 tablespoons
    Green peas ½ of can 15oz
    Banana 1

47. Sausage 6oz
    Hummus jar 10oz
    Tomatoes fresh 2
    Red pepper sweet 1
    Green peas ½ of can 15oz

Rotisserie Chicken Recipes

48. Rotisserie chicken ½
    Cheese pepper jack 2oz

    Tangerines 3
    Cranberry souse 2 tablespoons

49. Rotisserie chicken ½
    Artichoke Hearts marinated 6oz
    Beans ½ of can 15.5oz
    Tomatoes 2
    Red pepper sweet 1

50. Rotisserie chicken ½
    Mushrooms marinated 4.5oz
    Tomatoes 2
    Olives black ½ of can 6oz

Ham Recipes

51. Ham 4oz
Raspberry 6oz
Cucumber fresh medium size
Corn sweet ½ of can 15.25oz
Red pepper sweet 1

52. Ham 4oz
Cranberry souse 2 tablespoons
Tangerines 3
Cheese Queso Oaxaca 2oz
Salad Iceberg Garden 10oz

53. Ham 4oz
Avocados 2
Cucumber fresh medium size
Olives black ½ of can 6oz

54. Ham 4oz
Beans ½ of can 15.5oz
Bananas 2
Corn sweet ½ of can 15.25oz
Crackers 10

55. Ham 4oz
Pineapple ½
Tomatoes 2
Corn sweet ½ of can 15.25oz
Cranberry souse 2 tablespoons

Cooked Turkey Meat Recipes

56. Turkey meat cooked 5oz
Mangos 2
Cucumber fresh medium size
Red Pepper sweet 1
Spinach 10oz

57. Turkey meat cooked 5oz
Mushrooms marinated 4.5oz
Tangerines 2
Potato salad 4 tablespoons

58. Turkey meat cooked 5oz
Beats marinated 5 slices
Beans ½ of can 15.5oz
Cucumber fresh medium size

59. Smoked turkey meat 5oz
Cucumber fresh medium size
Red pepper sweet 1
Salad Iceberg Garden 10oz

Pastrami Recipes

60. Pastrami 5oz
    Cheese Mozzarella smoked 4oz
    Cucumber fresh medium size
    Olives black ½ of can 6oz

61. Pastrami 5oz
    Tomatoes 2
    Tangerines 2
    Celery ½ of stem

62. Pastrami 5oz
    Artichoke Hearts marinated 6oz
    Red pepper sweet 1
    Herb Salad 2 cups

63. Pastrami 5oz
    Beats marinated 7 slices
    Cheese Mozzarella 4oz
    Olives black ½ of can 6oz

Beef Recipe

64. Beef 5oz
    Plums 3
    Cheese Gouda 3oz
    King's Hawaiian bread 4 bans

Hummus Recipes

65. Hummus 1 jar 10oz
    Artichoke Hearts marinated 6oz
    Cucumber fresh medium size
    King's Hawaiian bread 4 bans

66. Hummus 1 jar 10oz
    Sausage 6oz
    Olives black ½ of can 6oz
    Corn sweet ½ of can 15.25oz

67. Hummus 1 jar 10oz
    Cheese Mozzarella smoked 4oz
    Sauerkraut 2 tablespoons
    Onion white small size

68. Hummus 1jar 10oz
    Peaches 3
    Tangerines 3
    Chocolate 2oz

69. Hummus 1 jar 10oz
    Rotisserie chicken ½
    Mushrooms marinated 4.5oz
    Tomatoes 3

Cheese Recipes

70. Cheese Gouda 3oz
    Tangerines 3
    Red pepper sweet 1
    Green Peas ½ of can 15oz

71. Cheese Mozzarella smoked 8oz
    Tomatoes 3
    Olives black ½ of can 6oz
    Corn sweet ½ of can 15.25oz

72. Cheese Mozzarella smoked 8oz
    Artichoke Hearts marinated 6oz
    Hummus 1 jar 10oz
    Green peas ½ of can 15oz
    Red pepper 1 sweet

73. Cheese Mozzarella smoked 8oz
    Avocados 3
    Olives black ½ of can 6oz
    Green peas ½ of can 15oz
    Onion white small size

74. Cheese Gouda 4oz
    Bananas 2
    Corn sweet ½ of can 15.25oz
    Celery ½ of stem

75. Cheese Mozzarella 10oz
    Artichoke Hearts marinated 6oz
    Cucumber fresh small size
    Red pepper sweet 1
    Corn sweet ½ of can 15.25oz

76. Cheese Gouda 6oz
    Peaches 4
    Mango 4
    Croissants 2

77. Cheese Cottage 15oz
    Croissants 2
    Honey 1 tablespoon
    Strawberries 6oz
    Honeydew ½

78. Cheese spread 4oz
    Celery ½ of stem
    Mayonnaise 2 tablespoons
    Crackers 10
    Garlic 1 clove

79. Cheese spread 4oz
    Cucumber fresh 1 small size
    Olives black ½ can of 6oz
    Red pepper sweet 1 clove

80. Cheese spread 4oz
    Bread 2 slices
    Mayonnaise 2 tablespoons
    Garlic 1 clove

81. Cheese spread 4oz
    Cranberry souse 2 tablespoons
    Peaches 3
    Red pepper sweet 1

Sauer cream Recipes

82. Sauer cream 8oz
King's Hawaiian bread 4 bans
Onion white small size
Salt (your taste)

83. Sauer cream 8oz
Radish 1 bunch
Bread 2 slices
Onion white small size

Yogurt Recipes

84. Plain yogurt 12oz
    Tangerines 3
    Grapes ½ of 1LB
    Red pepper sweet 1
    Crackers 10 pieces

85. Plain yogurt 12oz
    Cucumber fresh medium size
    Red pepper sweet 1
    Celery ½ of stem

86. Plain yogurt 12oz
    Orange 1
    Honey 2 tablespoons
    Crackers 10 pieces

87. Plain yogurt 12oz
    Tomatoes 2
    Cheese Gouda 2oz
    Olives black ½ of can 6oz

88. Plain yogurt 12oz
    Cranberry souse 2 tablespoons
    Raspberries fresh 6oz
    King's Hawaiian bread 4 bans

89. Plain yogurt 12oz
    Beats marinated 7 slices
    Artichoke Hearts marinated 6oz
    Onion white small size

90. Plain yogurt 12oz
    Tomatoes 3
    Honey 2 tablespoons
    King's Hawaiian bread 4 bans

Sauerkraut Recipes

91. Sauerkraut 5oz
    Artichoke Hearts marineted 6oz
    Cucumber fresh medium size
    Red pepper sweet 1
    Olives black ½ of can 6oz

92. Sauerkraut 5oz
    Avocados 2
    Artichoke Hearts marinated 6oz
    Apple 2
    Corn sweet ½ of can 15.25oz

93. Sauerkraut 5oz
    Cranberry souse 2 tablespoons
    Corn sweet ½ of can 15.25oz
    Crackers 12 pieces

94. Sauerkraut 5oz
    Cucumber fresh medium size
    Olives black ½ of can 6oz
    Green peas ½ of can 15oz
    Onion white small size

95. Sauerkraut 5oz
    Tangerines 3
    Red pepper sweet 1
    Olives black ½ of can 6oz

96. Sauerkraut 5oz
    Beans ½ of can 15.5oz
    Red pepper sweet 1
    Onion white small size

Beans Recipes

97. Beans ½ of can 15.5oz
    Tomatoes 3
    Cheese Gouda 2oz
    Cucumber fresh medium size

98. Beans ½ of can 15.5oz
    Artichoke Hearts marinated 6oz
    Sausage 6oz
    Onion white small size

99. Beans ½ of can 15.5oz
    Bananas 2
    Green peas ½ of can 15oz
    Bread 2 slices

100. Beans ½ of can 15.5oz
     King's Hawaiian bread 4 bans
     Cucumber fresh medium size
     Beats marinated 7 slices

Printed in the United States
by Baker & Taylor Publisher Services